The Little Book of Dens

by Lynne Garner
Illustrations by Steve Evans

LITTLE BOOKS WITH BIG IDEAS

Published 2013 by Featherstone Education, an imprint of Bloomsbury Publishing Plc
50 Bedford Square, London, WC1B 3DP
www.bloomsbury.com

ISBN 978-1-4081-9398-3

Text © Lynne Garner 2013
Illustrations © Steve Evans
Cover photographs © London Early Years Foundation and Shutterstock

A CIP record for this publication is available from the British Library.
All rights reserved. No part of this publication may be reproduced in any form or by any means – graphic, electronic, or mechanical, including photocopying, recording, taping or information storage or retrieval systems – without the prior permission in writing of the publishers.

Printed and bound in Great Britain by Latimer Trend & Company Limited

1 3 5 7 9 10 8 6 4 2

This book is produced using paper that is made from wood grown in managed, sustainable forests. It is natural, renewable and recyclable. The logging and manufacturing process conform to the environmental regulations of the country of origin.

To see our full range of titles visit
www.bloomsbury.com

Contents

Introduction	**4–8**
Pirate Ship	9
Space Station	12
Writer's Room	15
Beach Hut	18
Big Balloon	21
Farm Barn	24
Steam Train	27
Spy HQ	30
Jungle Tent	33
Mad Scientist's Lab	36
Haunted House	39
Puppet Theatre	43
Artist's Studio	46
Greenhouse	49
Underwater Cave	52
Bandstand	55
Castle Keep	58
Roman Villa	62
Tree House	65

Introduction

The Little Book of Dens contains 19 different themes for den-making ideas. Each theme is supported by suggestions for imaginative play, games and activities, making this book ideal for those working in the early years setting.

How to use this book

> "Children need to play - it is part of their world that helps to develop their imagination, communication and understanding."
> Diane Rich, www.richlearningopportunities.co.uk - Nursery Education 2005

By encouraging den play, you are fulfilling the following 12 features of play as outlined in 'Learning Through Play: Babies, Toddlers and the Foundation Years' by Tina Bruce:

- Using first-hand experiences
- Making up rules
- Making props
- Choosing to play
- Rehearsing the future
- Pretending
- Playing alone
- Having a personal agenda
- Being deeply involved
- Trying out recent learning
- Co-ordinating ideas, feelings and relationships for free-flow play.

The themed dens in this book are based on topics that children will find both fun and educational, and will encourage children to explore imaginative play as well as experience learning opportunities. Each themed den idea is broken down into clear sections:

- What you need
- Make and dress your den
- Props and costume

▶ Activities and games

▶ Health and safety tips (where appropriate)

The What you need section lists the resources required for each part of the themed den play. These resources are inexpensive and easy to obtain. However, if you are unable to locate all items listed then play can easily be adapted to suit the items you have sourced.

Resources:
Tina Bruce (2001) 'Learning Through Play: Babies, Toddlers and the Foundation Years'. Hodder and Stoughton (page 117).

The Early Learning Goals

When encouraging children to play, it is important to support all areas of the learning experience. By providing ideas for den play, this book ensures that all sections of the revised EYFS framework are covered. The prime areas and specific areas of the curriculum are broken down into a further seven areas in total, these being:

Prime areas:
▶ Communication and Language (CL)

▶ Physical Development (PD)

▶ Personal, Social and Emotional Development (PSED)

Specific areas:
▶ Literacy (L)

▶ Mathematics (M)

▶ Understanding the World (UW)

▶ Expressive Arts and Design (EAD)

The themes, activities and games included in this book aim to fulfill all seven areas of the EYFS as outlined below.

Communication and Language (CL)
Listening and attention
Children listen attentively in a range of situations. They listen to stories, accurately anticipate key events and respond to what they hear with relevant comments, questions and actions. They give their attention to what others say and respond appropriately, while engaged in another activity.

Understanding
Children follow instructions involving several ideas or actions. They answer 'how' and 'why' questions about their experiences and in response to stories and events.

Speaking
Children express themselves effectively, showing awareness of listeners' needs. They use past, present and future forms accurately when talking about events that have happened or are to happen in the future. They develop their own narrative and explanations by connecting ideas and events.

Physical Development (PD)
Moving and handling
Children show good control and co-ordination in large and small movements. They move confidently in a range of ways, safely negotiating space. They handle equipment and tools effectively, including pencils for writing.

Health and self-care
Children know the importance for good health of physical exercise, and a healthy diet, and talk about ways to keep healthy and safe. They manage their own basic hygiene and personal needs successfully, including dressing and going to the toilet independently.

Personal, Social and Emotional Development (PSED)
Self-confidence and self-awareness
Children are confident to try new activities, and say why they like some activities more than others. They are confident to speak in a familiar group, will talk about their ideas, and will choose the resources they need for their chosen activities. They say when they do or don't need help.

Managing feelings and behaviour
Children talk about how they and others show feelings, talk about their own and others behaviour and its consequences, and know that some behaviour is unacceptable. They work as part of a group or class, and understand and follow the rules. They adjust their behaviour to different situations, and take changes of routine in their stride.

Making relationships
Children play co-operatively, taking turns with other. They take account of one another's ideas about how to organise their activity. They show sensitivity to others' needs and feelings, and form positive relationships with adults and other children.

Literacy (L)
Reading
Children read and understand simple sentences. They use phonic knowledge to decode regular words and read them aloud accurately. They also read some common irregular words. They demonstrate understanding when talking with others about what they have read.

Writing
Children use their phonic knowledge to write words in ways, which match their spoken sounds. They also write some irregular common words. They write simple sentences, which can be read by themselves and others. Some words are spelt correctly and others are phonetically plausible.

Mathematics (M)
Numbers
Children count reliably with numbers from 1 to 20, place them in order and say which number is one more or one less than a given number. Using quantities and objects, they add and subtract two single-digit numbers and count on or back to find the answer. They solve problems, including doubling, halving and sharing.

Shape, space and measures
Children use everyday language to talk about size, weight, capacity, position, distance, time and money to compare quantities and objects to solve problems. They recognise, create and describe patterns. They explore characteristics of everyday objects and shapes and use mathematical language to describe them.

Understanding the world (UW)
People and communities
Children talk about past and present events in their own lives and in the lives of family members. They know that other children don't always enjoy the same things, and are sensitive to this. They know about similarities and differences between themselves and others, and among families, communities and traditions.

The world
Children know about similarities and differences in relation to places, objects, materials and living things. They talk about the features of their own immediate environment and how environments might vary from one another. They make observations of animals and plants and explain why some things occur, and talk about changes.

Technology
Children recognise that a range of technology is used in places such as homes and schools. They select and use technology for particular purposes.

Expressive arts and design (EAD)
Exploring and using media and materials
Children sing songs, make music and dance, and experiment with ways of changing them. They safely use and explore a variety of materials, tools and techniques, experimenting with colour, design, texture, form and function.

Being imaginative
Children use what they have learnt about media and materials in original ways, thinking about uses and purposes. They represent their own ideas, thoughts and feelings through design and technology, art, music, dance, role-play and stories.

For each of the themed dens, the children will automatically fulfill many of the EYFS outcomes across many of the different sections. For example, when collecting the items needed they will choose the resources they need for their chosen activities (PSED). As they build the den they will play co-operatively and take account of one another's ideas (PSED), and handle equipment and tools effectively (PD). During imaginative play they will give their attention to what others say and respond appropriately (CL), and will select and use technology for particular purposes (UW). During the suggested activities they will demonstrate understanding when talking with others about what they have read (L); they may talk about size, weight, time, money etc. and explore characteristics of everyday objects (M). The children will also take part in singing songs, making music, dancing and experimenting with ways of changing them (EAD) and show good control and co-ordination in large and small movements (PD). Finally, they will read and understand simple sentences and use their phonic knowledge to write words (L).

Source:
'Development Matters in the Early Years Foundation Stage (EYFS), The British Association for Early Childhood Education', www.early-education.org.uk

Additional resources:
'Learning Through Play in the Early Years': The Early Years Interboard Panel - www.nicurriculum.org.uk

'Play and the Revised EYFS': introduction by Anne O'Connor, Community Playthings - www.communityplaythings.co.uk

Pirate Ship

Children love to play pirates. A den based on a pirate ship is sure to be a hit! To add to the fun, encourage everyone to choose a pirate name, for example, Captain Cutlass, Pirate Polly and Jolly Joe.

Make and dress your den:

What you need:
- Sheets and rope or cable ties
- Jolly Roger flag
- Sea-themed toys, e.g. crabs, fish, dolphins etc.
- Box to serve as a sea chest
- Pirate-themed music or sea sounds and device to play them on
- Balance bench

What you do:
1. Choose your area or room that is to be turned into a pirate ship.
2. Drape the sheets (to simulate the sails) and tie in place with the rope.
3. Above the entrance hang the Jolly Roger flag or signs, and decorate the area with pirate-themed items.
4. To add atmosphere, play the sea-themed sounds as background noise. If room allows, set up a balance bench to serve as a plank!

Props and costumes:

What you need:
- Loose trousers and striped T-shirt
- Piece of fabric to tie around your waist
- Waistcoat
- Bandana and hat
- Moustache or beard
- Face paints
- Toy spyglass
- Card, glue, elastic, scissors and tin foil

What you do:
1. Prior to setting up the den encourage the children to create a sign telling visitors, "Enter at ye own risk – Pirate Den." Also encourage them to write banners using pirate-like words, such as "Shiver me timbers", "Ahoy there, shipmates!" and "Aye aye, Captain."
2. Make eye patches from card by cutting an oval shape and folding it in half. Place glue inside the folded card, position the centre of the elastic along the crease and press flat. Once the glue has dried tie the elastic around the head, ensuring a good fit.
3. Create cutlasses using thick card and wrap with tin foil.

Activities and Games:

What you need:
Treasure Hunt!
- Foil-covered chocolate coins

Picnic
- Selection of picnic food

Treasure Map
- Large sheet of paper
- Tea bags
- Large bowl or sink, and water
- Matches
- Pens/pencils

What you do:
Treasure Hunt!
Hide foil-covered chocolate coins in a safe area and set the children on the task of finding the 'booty'.

Picnic
Rename foods, for example, 'chicken nuggets' become 'nuggets of gold', 'egg and cress' sandwich becomes 'seagull egg with seaweed', 'fruit squash' becomes 'grog.'

Treasure Map
Create 'parchment' for the map by soaking a large piece of paper in a weak solution of tea. Allow it to dry, then carefully burn the edges (adult only) and crumple. Once you have smoothed the paper out, it is ready for the children to add their map!

Useful links for additional resources:
- www.talklikeapirate.com - official site of 'Talk Like A Pirate' day
- www.teachingideas.co.uk - type 'pirate' in the search field
- www.busybeekidscrafts.com - scroll down to the list and click on 'pirate'
- www.freesound.org - downloadable free sounds

Health and safety tips:
- Make appropriate changes to the food if any of the children have intolerances or allergies.

Space Station

Children love the idea of space and space travel, making this an ideal theme to encourage imaginative play.

Make and dress your den:

What you need:
- Black fabric or sheets
- Rope or large pegs
- Space-themed toys, e.g. spaceships, aliens etc.
- Homemade play items, e.g. experiment box, constellation torch etc.
- Paper plates
- Tin foil
- Paper, colouring pencils, scissors, glue

What you do:
1. Choose an appropriate area, drape the fabric and tie in place with the rope or pegs.
2. Attach the portholes (see 'Props and costumes') randomly to the sheets on the inside of the den.
3. Dress the den with the space-themed toys and items made in activities.

Props and costumes:

What you need:
- Silver or grey trousers, tops and boots
- Boxes of various sizes
- Silver or grey paint, paintbrushes and paint tray
- Pipe cleaners
- Plastic bottle tops
- PVA glue
- Old electrical remotes (to act as scientific devices)

What you do:
1. Space suit: can be created from silver or grey clothes.
2. Space helmet: cut a hole in an appropriate size box, paint with silver or grey paint and add extras e.g. antenna and control buttons.
3. Portholes: prior to setting up create portholes. Simply cut out the middle of the plate and cover with foil. Draw a space picture on the paper (to fit inside the hole) and stick behind the plate.
4. Control panel: use a suitable box, paints, glue and various found items to create a control panel for imaginative play.

Activities and Games:

What you need:
Moon Sand
- 4 cups of play sand
- 2 cups of corn flour
- 1 cup of water
- Large bowl and mixing spoon

Experiment Box
- Large cardboard box
- Rubber gloves
- Scissors and sticky tape
- Clear plastic
- Small items, e.g. stones, shells etc.

Explore the Constellations
- ▶ Torch
- ▶ Constellation maps
- ▶ Paper, pin and elastic band

What you do:

Moon Sand
Mix together the ingredients. Encourage the children to squeeze and pummel it and discuss how it feels. Should it dry out add a little water.

Experiment Box
Cut two holes in the side and poke rubber gloves through these holes. Fill with a range of play items, perhaps the play sand. Cover with a sheet of clear plastic and attach using the sticky tape.

Explore the Constellations
Print off some constellation maps (see 'Useful links for additional resources'), use a pin to create holes in the paper, and attach to the front of a torch with an elastic band.

Useful links for additional resources:

- ▶ www.kidsknowit.com - type 'constellation' in the search field
- ▶ funschool.kaboose.com - click 'globe-rider' then 'space'
- ▶ space.about.com/library/graphics/constellation_patterns.jpg - constellation maps

Writer's Room

A great den for encouraging children to explore and expand their imaginations and discover the joys of creative writing.

Make and dress your den:

What you need:
- Household furniture (sturdy, low books cases are ideal)
- Photographs (old family photographs would be perfect)
- Books
- Posters and toys of favourite book characters
- Bean bags and cushions
- Lap trays
- Pictures and interesting objects for inspiration

What you do:
1. Choose a quiet corner of a room and use items such as low, sturdy bookcases to create the walls of your den.
2. Stock the den area with books, then accessorise it using the items suggested above.

Props and costumes:

What you need:
- A small desk with a desk lamp
- Old-fashioned typewriter
- Black board and chalks
- Paper and pens/pencils
- Waste paper bin
- Dressing-up box, including spectacles, wigs, hats etc.

What you do:
1. Children could dress up as a favourite book character, or encourage them to discover famous authors, e.g. Enid Blyton, Roald Dahl, Beatrix Potter, Lewis Carroll and J. M. Barrie. They could create a costume based on the fashion worn at the time the author was writing.
2. Props would include items such as paper, pens, a typewriter etc.

Activities and Games:

What you need:
'What Happened Next?' game
- Storybooks

Torn Poem
- Newspaper/magazines
- Plain white paper
- Glue sticks

'Their name is...' game
- Photographs
- Paper and pens/pencils

What you do:
'What Happened Next?' game

Read a story, then ask the children what they think could have happened next. Older children can be encouraged to write their ideas whilst younger children can tell their story or draw their responses.

Torn Poem
Tear words and headings from the newspapers and magazines for children to stick onto plain paper and create their own poems.

'Their name is...' game
Provide the children with photographs. Older children can be encouraged to write about a person in the photograph, giving them a name, listing things they like and dislike, the name of their pet, etc. Younger children can be encouraged to talk about the person.

Useful links for additional resources:

- tlc.howstuffworks.com/family/writing-activities-for-kids.htm - writing activities
- www.enchantedlearning.com - type 'essay' in search field
- www.readingrockets.org/article/392/ - 25 writing and reading activities

Beach Hut

Everyone loves to spend a day on the beach – and what better way to enjoy it than to move into a beach hut for the day!

Make and dress your den:

What you need:
- Beach windshields
- Large sheet
- Rope, cable ties or large bulldog clips
- Rush beach mats and/or large beach towels
- Deck chairs
- Large beach umbrella
- Toys, e.g. fish/lobster/crabs etc.
- CD of sea sounds and device to play it on

What you do:
1. Outdoors: push the windshields into the ground forming a rectangle, remembering to leave a gap for the door. Indoors: tie the windshields to sturdy pieces of furniture using the rope or bulldog clips. Both: spread the sheet over the top and attach to the poles using cable ties or bulldog clips.
2. Cover the floor with rush beach mats and/or beach towels.
3. Dress with the sea/beach themed toys.
4. To add atmosphere, play the sea themed sounds as background noise.

Props and costumes:

What you need:
- Shorts and T-shirts
- Sun glasses and sun hats
- Beach balls, buckets and spades, lilos

What you do:
1. Encourage the children to dress in clothes they would wear to the beach.
2. Props can include items such as beach balls, beach inflatables, buckets and spades etc.

Activities and Games:

What you need:
Beach Treasure Hunt
- Stop watch
- Play pit with sand
- Small items to hide (seashells, toy jewellery, glass nuggets etc.)
- Bucket and spade per child

Jellyfish Art
- Paper plates
- Scissors and glue
- Paints or colouring pencils
- Tissue paper
- Googly eyes

Listen and Describe
▶ Large shell

What you do:

Beach Treasure Hunt
Prior to the game, hide items in the play pit sand. Set the stop watch then shout "GO!". At the same time, players dig for the hidden items using the spade. When they find an item they place it in the bucket. When the stopwatch beeps, digging stops and the player who found the most items is the winner.

Jellyfish Art
Cut a plate in half, decorate one side and attach the eyes. To create tentacles, tear strips of tissue paper and stick them along the straight edge.

Listen and Describe
Provide children with a large shell and encourage them to hold it to their ear. Older children can write about what they hear and what they associate the noise with, whilst younger children can draw their responses.

Useful links for additional resources:

▶ www.elcofnwflorida.org - click 'get involved' then type 'under the sea' in search field

▶ www.the-preschool-professor.com - type 'beach-themed' in the search field

▶ www.pinterest.com - type 'beach themed activities' in the search field

Health and safety tips:

▶ For outside play, encourage the children to wear a suitable sunscreen lotion and a hat.

Big Balloon

There's magic in a balloon ride, floating on the wind and seeing where it takes you. So encourage the children to explore this delightful form of transport with imaginative play.

Make and dress your den:

What you need:
- Table
- Bamboo screening
- Cable ties or bulldog clips
- Thick card
- Paint, paintbrushes and paint tray
- Scissors and glue
- String or rope
- Brown bags
- Large cushions

21

What you do:

1. Turn a table upside down and attach the bamboo screen around it, ensuring that you leave a gap or hole so the children can get in and out easily.
2. Cut out two balloon-shaped pieces of card. Encourage the children to decorate them.
3. In the first, cut a slot centrally from the top to the centre.
4. In the second, cut a slot centrally from the bottom and slot the two together. Glue if needed.
5. Hang the large cardboard balloon above the 'basket'.
6. Blow into the brown bags to inflate, tie at the top and tie around the basket.
7. Finally, cover the floor with cushions.

Props and costumes:

What you need:
- Cargo trousers and T-shirt
- Safari helmet or a bush hat
- Jacket with lots of pockets
- Satchel
- Water flask
- Compass and map
- Binoculars and camera
- Notepad and pencil or other recording device

What you do:

1. Conservationists use balloons to watch animals without disturbing them, whilst adventurers, explorers and photographers use them to take stunning landscape images. So encourage the children to become these people by wearing appropriate 'safari' type clothing.
2. Whilst on safari, your adventurers will want to make records of what they see, so arm them with the correct tools.

Activities and Games:

What you need:
Binoculars
- 2 cardboard tubes
- Paint, paintbrushes and paint tray
- PVA glue
- String

On Safari
- Camera
- Small plastic animals
- Small note pad and pencil

Mini Hot Air Balloons
- Balloons
- Small boxes
- Colouring pencils
- Sticky tape

What you do:
Binoculars

Decorate the outside of the tubes, stick them together and attach the string so it is long enough to go over the head.

On Safari

Place small plastic animals around the basket and encourage the children to pretend to take photographs, take notes or draw what they see.

Mini Hot Air Balloons

Blow up the balloon. Decorate the outside of the box and attach to the balloon. Hang around the room so your adventurers can take part in a balloon race.

Useful links for additional resources:
- www.kiwifamilies.co.nz - type 'hot air balloon' in the search field
- coolestfamilyontheblock.com - type 'hot air balloon' in the search field
- www.kathimitchell.com/balloons.htm - hot air balloon links

Farm Barn

Most children love animals, so encourage this enthusiasm by getting them to spend the day on a farm.

Make and dress your den:

What you need:
- Table
- Large sheets of cardboard
- Scissors
- Cable ties
- Felt-tip pens
- Hay
- Bundles or corn
- Play digging forks and spades
- Blankets
- Buckets
- Churns
- Toy farm animals (plush and plastic)
- Toy tractors etc.
- Farmyard sounds and device to play them on

I will need

What you do:
1. Encourage the children to draw the planks of wood that the barn is made of on the cardboard.
2. Fix this around four sides of the table, attaching in place using the cable ties.
3. Cut a door into one side (adult step).
4. Dress the inside with straw on the floor and some of the other props, e.g. plush toys, buckets, baskets etc.
5. To add atmosphere, play the farmyard sounds as background noise.

Props and costumes:

What you need:
- Trousers/jeans or dungarees and shirt
- Hat
- Waistcoat
- Wellingtons
- Walking stick or crook
- Basket
- Watering can and buckets

What you do:
1. There are a range of people the children could pretend to be. These include: farmer, shepherd, sheep-shearer, vet, tractor driver/mechanic. As most of these are hands-on jobs, clothes normally used for mucky play are a good idea!
    - Farmer/shepherd: walking stick or crook
    - Vet: white lab coat, small old suitcase, bandages, small bottles of 'ointment' etc.
    - Mechanic: toolbox, tools etc.

Activities and Games:

What you need:
Song Time
- Farm-themed song sheets
- Musical instruments

25

Story Time
- Farm-themed picture books

Memory Card Game
- Pictures of farm animals (two of each animal)
- Thin cards
- Scissors
- Dry glue stick
- Pen/pencil

What you do:

Song Time
Encourage the children to join in some farm-themed songs, e.g. 'Old MacDonald Had a Farm' or 'Oats and Beans and Barley Grow'.

Story Time
There are a large number of suitable farm-themed books.

Memory Card Game
Cut playing-card sized rectangles from the thin card. Cut out the animal images and stick each to a side of card. Write the name of the animal under each image. To play: shuffle the cards and place face down in rows. Each player takes it in turn to turn over two cards. If the images match, they keep the cards; if they do not, they turn them back over. Play continues until all the cards are used. The player with the most cards wins.

Useful links for additional resources:
- www.allkidsnetwork.com - type 'farm crafts' in the search field for craft activities
- www.activityvillage.co.uk - type 'farm animal games' in the search field for activities and games
- www.notimeforflashcards.com - in categories (right hand side, scroll down) click on 'farm' or 'farm animals'

Steam Train

Children of all ages seem to love stream trains. Encourage the children to have fun 'travelling' the world in their own train.

What you need:
- Large cardboard boxes
- Paper plates
- Thick, short cardboard tube
- Scissors
- Cotton wool
- Cushions

What you do:
1. Prior to the creation of the den, paint the boxes using images of trains as inspiration.
2. Use the largest box to create a carriage or the engine, cutting holes for windows and doors.
3. Attach the paper plates to represent wheels; again, decorate prior to making the train.
4. Attach the cardboard tube to create a funnel, using cotton wool to represent the steam.
5. Finally, add cushions or pillows for the travellers to sit on.

Props and costumes:

What you need:
Clothing for train employees:
- Black/dark trousers or long skirt
- Black or dark jacket
- White shirt or blouse
- Tie and hat

Clothing for passengers:
- Similar to above although brighter colours can be chosen
- Tail coat
- Top hat or bowler hat

Other props:
- Raffle tickets
- Toy till and play money
- Luggage
- Train timetable

What you do:
1. Props for train employees: raffle tickets, play till, play money, a whistle and two flags (red and green).
2. Props for passengers: luggage, train timetable, packed lunch etc.
3. Costume for employees: a stationmaster would wear a dark uniform with their job title or name on.
4. Costume for passengers: travel back in time to the golden age of steam and recreate a Victorian costume (see links opposite).

Activities and Games:

What you need:
- Cardboard tubes
- Paints, paintbrushes and paint tray
- Thin black card
- Cotton wool
- Scissors and glue
- Mini trains
- Whistle
- Red and green flags

What you do:

Imaginative play
Use the tickets and till to create a ticket office next to your train for imaginative play.

Mini trains
Paint the tubes. Whilst the paint dries, cut out four circles for the wheels and create a tube from the black card to form a funnel. Attach the funnel and the wheels to the tube. Finally, add cotton wool to the top of the funnel to represent the steam. Coaches can also be created in the same way – simply omit the funnel.

Become a signalman
Hold up the green flag in your left hand: this is the 'all-right' signal. Have the red flag in your right hand, and hold it up if there is a problem with the train. Also blow the whistle and shout phrases like 'all aboard!'

Useful links for additional resources:
- www.dltk-kids.com - type 'transport trains' in the search field
- www.youtube.com - type 'Victorian children' in the search field for costume ideas
- www.petersrailway.com - click 'how it works' and ' fun videos' for videos of train journeys

Spy HQ

In this den, players will be able to use their imagination and turn themselves in to the next super spy!

Make and dress your den:

What you need:
- Office screens or similar
- Blu-tac, glue and sticky tape
- Pens/pencils and paper
- Black ink-pad (suitable for use on skin)
- Note pad
- Cardboard files
- Old laptops
- Phones
- Desks and chairs
- In/out trays
- Maps

What you do:
1. Clear an area and position the office screens as needed.
2. Decorate as a high-tech office, using the office items listed in 'What you need'.

3. Place a large map on the wall with dots/names showing where operatives are based, where the villain's lair is, possible targets etc.
4. To 'dress' the outside of the den you'll need black signs with yellow lettering, with words such as: "Agents only", "Restricted access", "Top clearance required" and "Danger, keep out!"
5. To add atmosphere, play the sound of people talking as background noise.
6. Alternately, play spy-themed music from films such as 'Spy Kids', 'Harriet The Spy', 'Mission Impossible' and 'James Bond'.

Props and costumes:

What you need:
- Spy clothes: black or grey clothes including long coats, hats, spectacles etc.
- Spy kit: binoculars, magnifying glass, camera, tape recorder or similar, brief case etc.
- Disguises: assortment of dressing up clothes
- Recording of people talking and device to play it on
- Black and yellow warning signs: see 'Make and dress your den'
- Black card or fur fabric
- False eyelash glue: see 'Health and safety tips'

What you do:
Any dark clothes can be accessorised with long coats, hats and glasses to transform the children into spies in training! Items to use as disguises will also be required.

False beards and moustaches can be cut from black card or black fur fabric and attached using false eyelash glue: see 'Health and safety tips'.

Activities and Games:

What you need:
Covert Operation Game
- Tape/ribbon
- Blu tac
- Stopwatch

False Identities
- Thin white card

- Pens/pencils
- Passport-type photographs
- Dry glue sticks
- Rubber stamps

What you do:
Covert Operation Game
Create a maze, using tape to emulate the lazer beams that are used as motion detectors in vaults etc. Players time themselves for getting through the maze without touching the tape. The player with the fastest speed is the winner.

False Identities
Encourage the children to make new identities for themselves or someone else by creating passes, passports etc.

Hide and Seek
One player is the spy and the other is the baddie.

Code Communications
Children create their own codes: these can be used to pass secret messages to one another, or play a game of hunt the treasure where the clues are in code. The treasure is perhaps a stolen list of top-secret information, or an important new invention.

Useful links for additional resources:
- www.allfortheboys.com - click 'search' along the top, then type 'spy' into the search field
- www.topspysecrets.com - spy related activities (contains some advertising)
- www.ehow.com - type 'how to make spy gadgets for kids' for a list of fun ideas

Health and safety tips:
- When using items such a ink-pads for finger printing and gentle eyelash glue for attaching moustaches, carry out a small test patch on each child 24 hours prior to play to test for allergies.

Jungle Tent

It doesn't matter if you're an explorer or a conservationist when staying in the jungle – you'll always experience the fun and adventure of living in a tent!

Make and dress your den:

What you need:
- Curtain pole
- 'G' clamps
- Camouflage fabric
- Green/camouflage netting or similar
- Heavy items such as large books
- Green shower curtain
- Camp bed and camp lamp
- Small desk
- Potted and plastic plants

What you do:

1. Hang the curtain pole from the ceiling, fixing at either end. If this is not possible rest on sturdy, stable furniture and fix in place using 'G' clamps.
2. Drape the fabric over the curtain pole, pull out to make an 'A' shape and fix in place using heavy items.
3. Decorate further using camouflage netting.
4. To represent vines hanging across the entrance, cut the shower curtain into thick strips and hang over the door.
5. Place plants around the tent to create a jungle, and hide jungle animal toys in the plants.

Props and costumes:

What you need:
- Camouflage-coloured shorts, shirt and long green socks
- Walking boots
- Scarf
- Pith helmet

Props for Explorer
- Binoculars, map and compass
- Drinks bottle
- Rucksack
- 'Satellite' phone
- Pre-packed food

Props for Conservationist
- Note pads and pencils
- Microscope and binoculars
- Identification books/cards
- Rucksack
- Two-way radio

What you do:

Explorers and conservationists will wear similar costumes; however, their rucksacks will contain slightly different items (see above: 'What you need').

Activities and Games:

What you need:

"I know that animal!"
- Animal sounds and device to play them on

I Spy
- Selection of jungle-themed toy animals
- Stopwatch

Paper Plate Animals
- Paper plates
- Pens/pencils
- Scissors
- Glue

What you do:

"I know that animal!"

Play animal sounds and encourage the players to write down which animal they think each sound is made by. Younger children can put their hands up to answer. For each one they guess correctly they win a point. As the end of the game, the player with the most points wins the game.

I Spy

Hide animals around the tent and encourage the children to find as many as they can in an allotted time. The child who finds the most is the winner.

Paper Plate Animals

Use the materials to create a range of jungle animals. For ideas, visit the first link below.

Useful links for additional resources:

- www.firstpalette.com - type 'jungle' or 'paper plate animals' in the search field
- www.dltk-kids.com - click on 'animal crafts' then scroll down to 'jungle/rainforest animals'
- www.childfun.com - type 'jungle activity theme' in the search field

Mad Scientist's Lab

Science can seem like magic! Encourage the children to explore science and its wonders in their very own lab.

Make and dress your den:

What you need:
- Large white sheets
- Scientific instruments e.g. microscope, telescope, test tubes
- Science-themed books and posters
- Large paper towels (for cleaning 'chemical' spills)
- Warning signs (see 'Make and dress your den')
- Table and chairs

What you do:
1. Dress a small area of a room by hanging up white sheets and fixing in a suitable manner.
2. Place a table in the middle, containing scientific instruments and science-related books.
3. Put up science-themed posters (you can make your own) e.g. maps of the world, space, the water cycle etc.
4. Create signs with the words: "Danger - Keep Out", "Scientists Only Beyond This Point", "Experiments in Progress", "Top Secret" and "Goggles Must Be Worn!"

Props and costumes:

What you need:
- White lab coats or large white shirts
- Apron
- Goggles and rubber gloves
- Name/security tags
- Radioactive warning sign
- Paper and pens/pencils
- Stopwatch and clipboards

What you do:
1. Scientists should wear white lab coats and carry lots of pens in their pockets! They could also carry clipboards to make notes.
2. They'll also need a security tag and a radiation warning tag.
3. Whilst carrying out their experiments, the children should wear rubber gloves and goggles.

Activities and Games:

What you need:
Oobleck
- 1 cup of water
- 2 cups of corn starch
- Mixing bowl and large wooden spoon
- Rubber gloves

Visible Sound Waves
- Speaker
- Baking tray
- Food colouring
- Oobleck

Make your own Rain/ Rainbow
- Kettle, water and ice cubes
- Jar and plate
- Sheet of white paper

What you do:
Oobleck
This substance has the properties of both a solid and a liquid.
Mix the ingredients together in a bowl to create a paste.
Encourage experimentation with the mixture. If punched, the mixture acts as a solid, but if you gently push your hand into it then it becomes a liquid!

Visible Sound Waves
Place some Oobleck into the baking tray and rest the tray on the speaker. Turn on the sound and watch the Oobleck 'dance'. For additional fun, add a little food colouring, remembering to wear gloves to avoid staining hands.

Make Your Own Rain
Fill the jar one-third full with hot water (adult step). Place the plate on top of the jar and watch it fill with condensation. Place the ice cubes on the plate and watch as 'rain' runs down the insides of the jar.

Make Your Own Rainbow
On a sunny day, fill a jar with water and hold it up to the sun. Place a piece of paper below the jar and adjust until a rainbow of colours appears.

Useful links for additional resources:
- www.sciencekids.co.nz - click on 'experiments'
- www.weatherwizkids.com - weather-related games and experiments
- kids.nationalgeographic.co.uk - click on 'fun stuff' then 'science'

Haunted House

Being scared by ghosts, ghouls and monsters can be fun! Create a safe space where children can feel that thrill run down their spine.

Make and dress your den:

What you need:
- Table
- Cardboard boxes
- Paints
- Scissors
- Cable ties
- Black sheets, strips of cloth and wool
- Toy spiders, bats and other creepy crawlies
- Toy bones, skulls and skeletons
- Glow in the dark spooky shapes and eyes
- Spooky music and device to play it on

What you do:

1. Flatten the cardboard boxes and encourage the children to decorate them as a house. Once the paint is dry, position the cardboard house around the table legs and tape in place on the inside corners.
2. Drape sheets, strips of cloth and the spider's web wool across the inside of the house, and attach the spiders.
3. Create signs with scary sayings, such as "Boo!", "Got Ya!" and "Behind Youooo!"
4. Hang bats from the ceiling and attach the glow-in-the-dark scary shapes where appropriate.
5. To add atmosphere, play the spooky music as background noise.
6. Alternatively, decorate an entire room and dressing with the 'scary' themed items.

Props and costumes:

What you need:
Ghost
- White sheet with eyeholes
- Belt

Skeleton
- Old black clothes
- White paint and paintbrush

Monster
- Old clothes
- Old hats, scarves etc.
- Red paint and paintbrush
- Facepaints
- Wigs, glasses, 'hairy hands' gloves, false noses etc.

Ghost hunter
- Camping lamp, torch or electrical candles
- Camera and camcorder
- Old TV remote control (to serve as a ghost detector)
- Voice recorder
- Old-fashioned light meter
- Head torch
- Large rucksack

What you do:

1. Ghost hunters: children can wear their own clothes.
2. Ghost: cut holes at child's eye level, drape sheet over child and place a belt around the waist.
3. Skelton: paint bones onto black tops and trousers. Then use face paints to create a skull effect.
4. Monster: mix and match old clothes, ripping and adding red paint. Add wigs and use face paints to complete the effect!
5. Ghost hunters need to be able to detect those ghosts, so create a ghost hunting kit that contains cameras, light meters, heat sensors etc.

Activities and Games:

What you need:
Mummy Race
- Rolls of bandage (or cut an old sheet into strips)
- Stopwatch

Mini Ghosts
- Paper or plastic cups
- Cloth
- Black felt-tip pen
- String, scissors and large-eyed darning needle

Knock 'em flying!
- Cardboard tubes
- Paper, card, scissors
- PVA glue
- Paints/pencil
- Small ball

What you do:

Mummy Race

Place players in pairs and give each of them a couple of rolls of bandage. Set the stopwatch for two minutes and shout "GO!" One player wraps the other in the bandage. When the two minutes have ended, the pair who has created the best mummy costume is the winning team. For extra fun, make the removal of the wrappings another race game.

Mini Ghosts

Pierce a hole centrally in the base of the paper or plastic cup, cut out a circle of cloth and snip a small hole centrally in it. Cut a piece of string, tie a knot in one end and thread through the hole, so the knot is inside the cup. Thread the string through the middle of the cloth, so it drapes over the upside-down cup. Draw in the mouth and eyes then hang up.

Knock 'em flying!

Create ten cardboard tube monsters. Place them in a triangle on the ground (four in the back row, three in the next, two in the next and one at the front). Each player stands a couple of metres away and rolls the ball at the monsters. The number of monsters knocked over equals the number of points scored. Each player rolls the ball three times. The player with the highest score wins.

Useful links for additional resources:

- ▶ spoonful.com - type 'mask' or 'monster' in the search field
- ▶ www.identity33.com/mfb_giftbox.html - monster masks to download and colour in
- ▶ www.countryliving.com - type 'Halloween templates' in the search field

Puppet Theatre

This den is based on the tradition of **Punch and Judy** and encourages the children to learn through puppet play.

Make and dress your den:

What you need:
- 2 very large, rigid cardboard boxes
- Paints, paintbrushes and paint tray
- Duct tape or similar and scissors
- Large sheets of thick white card
- Pens/pencils
- Stick-on Velcro
- Large comfortable pillows and blankets, or deck chairs

What you do:
1. Choose two very large boxes that are the same size and shape.
2. Paint the outsides of the two boxes with thick vertical stripes.
3. Once the paint has dried, cut the flaps off the lids of both boxes, so that one side of each is left open. Turn one of the boxes upside down so that the exposed side is on the floor; keep the other box upright, with the exposed side at the top.

4. Cut a rectangular hole in the side of the upside down box, to create the window for the puppet theatre. If the box is rectangular, choose one of the long sides. This will form the front of the theatre.
5. With the second box, cut a child-sized door out of one of the sides. Again, if the box is rectangular, choose one of the long sides. This will form the back of the theatre.
6. Stack the first box, with the window and the exposed base, on top of the second box with the door and exposed top, so that the theatre window is on the top at the front and the door is on the bottom at the back, with a space to stand inside the theatre.
7. Check that this last box is around head height (if not, add a strip of cardboard in between the two to add height) and secure all in place with duct tape.
8. Your characters will need a backdrop to 'act' against! Cut the thick white card so that it will fit inside the back of the top box. Encourage the children to decorate the backdrop. You could create multiple backdrops, each on a different piece of card, for different scenarios.
9. To attach, use the stick-on Velcro so that when it is in position the backdrop can be seen though the front window.
10. If your puppets are going to perform to an audience, place pillows, blankets or deck chairs in front of the box.

Alternative idea:
Cut a hole in a sheet at the correct height and drape across a doorway.

Props and costumes:

What you need:
- White lab coats or large white shirts
- Apron
- Goggles and rubber gloves
- Name/security tags
- Radioactive warning sign
- Paper and pens/pencils
- Stopwatch and clipboards

What you do:
1. Stage hands: those working behind the scenes should wear black clothes.
2. Audience: can wear everyday clothes.

3. Usherette: simply add an apron over their own clothes. They'll need an usherette's tray: create one tray by attaching a length of webbing or a canvas strap to the tray that can go over the head and one shoulder.

Activities and Games:

What you need:
Imaginative Play
- Raffle tickets
- Money
- Programme

Posters and Programmes
- Paper and thin card
- Pen/pencils and scissors

Puppets
- Socks
- Pom-poms
- Knitting yarn
- Googly eyes
- PVA glue
- Felt and other craft materials

What you do:

Imaginative play
Encourage the children to enjoy imaginative play by putting on a show! Sell tickets and act to an audience. Raffle tickets can be used as seat tickets, and an 'usherette' can sell real or imaginary drinks and snacks.

Posters and Programmes
The children can create their own posters and programmes.

Puppets
Using the links below, the children can be encouraged to make their own puppets.

Useful links for additional resources:
- www.kidspot.com.au - finger puppet templates
- www.firstpalette.com - type 'puppets' in the search field
- www.ichild.co.uk - click on 'puppets' in the subject listing

Artist's Studio

Encourage your budding artists to enjoy and experiment with all manner of art forms in the safety of their own studio.

Make and dress your den:

What you need:
- Shower curtains
- Methods of hanging
- Easy to clean table and chairs
- Posters, e.g. of famous artists, art, colour wheels etc.
- Blue-tac or sticky tape
- Personal items for inspiration, e.g. pictures of family/friends, favourite toys etc.

What you do:

1. Choose an area with an easy-clean floor, then hang the curtains to form a 'room'.
2. Place the table and chairs in the middle.
3. Dress your den with inspirational posters of famous artists and their work.
4. Leave space for your artists to show their work.
5. Add items such as an easel, articulated models, brushes in pots etc.

Props and costumes:

What you need:
- Large old shirt, baggy trousers or long skirt
- Scruffy shoes
- Beret
- Moustaches
- Apron
- Artist's palette and easel
- Artist's articulated wooden models

What you do:

1. As the children will be enjoying art and craft-related activities, clothes suitable for mucky play should be worn or else a wipeable apron over everyday clothes. Alternatively, encourage them to wear the archetypal white shirt with beret.
2. Props will include items to be used and created in the activities.

Activities and Games:

What you need:
Dressing Up
- Selection of clothes and accessories

Exploring Colour
- Paper
- Paints, paintbrushes and paint tray
- Colourful items such as leaves

3D Art
- Air-dry clay and clay tools

47

Found Art
- Cardboard boxes
- Egg boxes
- Old CDs
- Bubble wrap
- Fabric

What you do:

Dressing Up
Help the children to dress up as a character from a picture or a famous artist. See links below for ideas.

Exploring Colour
Encourage the children to mix as many different shades of one colour as they can and paint a picture with it. Alternatively, challenge them to collect items that are different shades of the same colour, e.g. leaves and grasses, and create a collage. Once complete, support the children as they count the number of different shades and discuss the concept of colour and shades.

3D Art
Help the children to create a piece of 3D art using clay and tools.

Found Art
Encourage the children to use the found items to create their own art.

Useful links for additional resources:
- www.teachingideas.co.uk - click on the 'art' button for art ideas/resources
- www.activityvillage.co.uk - click on 'craft' for themed art/craft ideas
- ohhappyday.com - type 'little artists costumes' in the search field for dressing-up ideas
- www.incredibleart.org - type 'dress up' in the search field for dressing up ideas

Health and safety tips:
- If you pick leaves etc., ensure the children wash their hands afterwards to ensure they do not ingest anything unsuitable.
- Some children may have a slight allergy to clay and other 'wet' items, so they may need to wear gloves.

Greenhouse

Help the children to learn about all things that grow, by creating their very own greenhouse.

Make and dress your den:

What you need:
- 4 poles
- Large sheet of clear plastic and cable ties
- Table and garden chairs
- Items you will be using for the activities (see overleaf)
- Gardening books

What you do:
1. Push the poles into the ground.
2. Wrap the plastic sheeting around three sides and tie in place. For safety reasons, do not drape a sheet over the top as a roof.
3. Set up a table for activities, with a few garden chairs.
4. Dress your den with the items you'll be using for the activities plus posters showing beneficial garden insects and animals, such as hedgehogs.
5. Add a few books related to the theme of 'gardening and growing'.

Props and costumes:

What you need:
- ▶ Wear suitable clothes for outside mucky play
- ▶ You may wish to add a hat, sunscreen, gloves and an apron
- ▶ Items you will be using for the activities (see below)

What you do:

1. As the children will be enjoying art and craft-related activities, clothes suitable for mucky play should be worn or else a wipeable apron over everyday clothes. Alternatively, encourage them to wear the archetypal white shirt with beret.
2. Props will include items to be used and created in the activities.

Activities and Games:

What you need:

Nature Prints
- ▶ Leaves
- ▶ Paint, paint tray and foam roller
- ▶ Paper

Mini Garden
- ▶ Seed tray, soil and seedlings
- ▶ Small plastic toys

Eggheads
- ▶ Eggs cups
- ▶ Washed eggshells
- ▶ Cotton wool
- ▶ Cress seeds
- ▶ Stickers
- ▶ Pens

What you do:

Nature Prints

Cover the backs of leaves with paint and place onto a piece of paper, paint side down. Place another piece of paper on top and gently press. Remove the paper and the leaf to reveal the print left behind.

Mini Garden
Fill the seed tray with soil, then plant the seedlings. Now inhabit this new mini garden with the small plastic toys. You may wish to theme, e.g. dinosaurs for your own Jurassic park!

Eggheads
Decorate the eggshells. Place a small amount of cotton wool inside the eggshell then sprinkle it with cress seeds. Use an eggcup to hold the eggshell upright in a draft free, well-lit position and wait for the cress to grow. Keep on eye on the cotton wool, and if it dries out add a little water.

Useful links for additional resources:
- www.bbc.co.uk/gardening - scroll down and click 'gardening with children' on the right hand side for activities
- www.gardeningwithchildren.co.uk - ideas and advice for safe play and learning
- www.netmums.com - click on 'activities' then 'garden'
- www.hedgehogstreet.org - information on hedgehogs!

Health and safety tips:
- When playing outside, it is always advisable to use an appropriate sunscreen and wear a hat.

Underwater Cave

Encourage the children to create their own underwater cave where they can discover the wildlife that inhabits our seas and oceans!

Make and dress your den:

What you need:
- 3 chairs
- Black sheet
- Items to weigh down fabric, e.g. books
- Green shower curtain or similar
- Scissors and wide sticky tape
- Shells
- Sea-themed plush/plastic toys
- Cushions
- Nylon thread
- Small suction pads

What you do:
1. Place the three chairs back to back, with enough room in between for play.
2. Drape with the fabric, leaving one side open.
3. Weigh down the edges of the fabric using books or other heavy objects.

4. Cut the green shower curtain into wide strips and drape across the front opening. Stick in place using the sticky tape.
5. Dress the inside of your cave with the cushions and some of the toys.
6. To achieve the feeling that you are at the bottom of the sea, suspend some of the toys from the classroom ceiling using the nylon thread and suction pads.
7. To add atmosphere, play the underwater sounds as background noise.

Props and costumes:

What you need:
- Swim suits
- Snorkel, flippers (diver)
- Large boots, sea helmet (deep-sea diver)
- Underwater-type music or sounds e.g. whales songs and device to play them on
- Camera
- Ocean life identification book

What you do:
1. Adventurers: beach-type clothes, including shorts and swimwear.
2. Divers: use black trousers and a tight fitting top. Add a mask and create your own set of air tanks (see below).
3. Deep-sea divers: dress in clothes listed above and create yourself a deep-sea helmet (see below).
4. Props could include a camera, compass, torch and small net for putting found items in.

Activities and Games:

What you need:
Air Tanks
- Circular crisp tubs
- Tin foil
- PVA glue
- Webbing or tape
- Bottle tops

53

Deep-Sea Diver's Helmet
- Cardboard box (large enough to fit over head)
- Small paper bowls
- Scissors
- Grey paint, paintbrushes and paint tray
- PVA glue
- Pipe cleaners

Snap Cards
- Sea animal photographs (two of each animal)
- Thin card
- Glue stick and scissors

What you do:

Air Tanks
Cover two crisp tubes with tin foil, or paint with grey or silver paint. Stick the tubes together and add bottle tops at one end to act as the valves. Attach webbing or tape to create two loops, so they can be worn over the shoulders.

Deep-Sea Diver's Helmet
Cut a hole in one side of the box (this will be the front) then cut a curve in either side, so the box will sit on the shoulders. Cut a hole in the base of three paper bowls. Create a criss-cross pattern over these holes using the pipe cleaners. Attach these to the side and top and paint the entire thing with grey paint.

Snap Cards
Cut the thin card into playing-card sized rectangles. Glue the images of the sea animals onto them. Under the images write the name of the animal. Create two of each card and use for a game of Snap.

Useful links for additional resources:
- www.pinterest.com - type 'under the sea' in the search field for craft ideas
- www.preschoolexpress.com - click on 'theme station' then on 'summer/oceans' for craft ideas
- funschool.kaboose.com - click on 'globe rider' then 'under the sea' for craft ideas and activities

Bandstand

Children love to listen and make music, so indulge this love and encourage your musicians by helping them to create their own bandstand.

Make and dress your den:

What you need:
- Cardboard boxes
- Paint, paintbrushes and paint tray
- Sticky tape and scissors
- Large garden umbrella with base
- Chairs and cushions
- Bunting

What you do:
1. Open out the cardboard boxes and decorate one side of each.
2. Once the paint has dried, stick the flattened boxes together and place in a large circle, with the decorated sides facing outwards, leaving a gap to serve as a door. Use the flaps of any of the boxes as a surface to allow you to weigh down the bandstand with heavy books etc.
3. Place the umbrella and base centrally inside the circle and open.
4. Dress with bunting, place chairs inside and scatter cushions outside for your audience.
5. Finally, add music stands with sheet music.

Props and costumes:

What you need:
- Trousers and smart jacket
- Gloves and hat
- Gold braid or ribbon
- Feathers
- Needle and thread, scissors
- Baton
- Music stands and sheet music
- Big band music CD and device to play it
- Variety of instruments, including homemade (see below)

What you do:
1. Bands dress in a uniform, so make your own by adding gold braid or ribbon to a smart jacket.
2. Hats are often worn, so trim with gold braid or ribbon and perhaps add a feather.
3. Those in the band should have instruments, and the conductor should hold a baton.
4. Those sitting in the audience could have drinks etc.

Activities and Games:

What you need:
Tambourine
- Paper plates
- Dry rice
- PVA glue
- Colouring pencils or paint and paintbrushes
- Clothes pegs

Kazoo
- Cardboard tubes
- Waxed paper
- Elastic bands
- Scissors
- Stickers

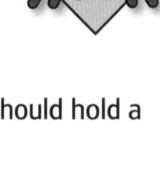

Compose your own song 1
- Radio
- Pencils and paper

Compose your own song 2
- Radio
- Pencils and paper
- Lyrics from nursery rhymes
- Glue stick and scissors

What you do:

Tambourine
Decorate the underside of two paper plates. Put the dry rice on one plate. Place a good amount of glue around the outer edge and then position the second plate on top of the first. Hold together with the clothes pegs whilst the glue dries.

Kazoo
Decorate a cardboard tube. Cut a piece of wax paper and pierce it with a couple of holes. Attach over one end with an elastic band. To play: hum into the other open end.

Compose your own song 1
Turn on the radio and flick between stations. As different songs are heard, children should write down one or two lyrics that they hear. When enough words have been 'collected', use them to create a new song.

Compose your own song 2
Cut up nursery rhyme lyrics from several different rhymes or songs. Rearrange the words and stick them onto paper in a different order to create a new song.

Useful links for additional resources:
- www.nancymusic.com - click on 'activities'
- www.satisfied-mind.com - ideas for making instruments, song sheets etc.
- www.mudcat.org/kids - simple instruments to make from found items

Castle Keep

Legends of kings, queens, knights and dragons usually feature a castle. Encourage the children to explore this magical world and create their own castle keep.

Make and dress your den:

What you need:
- Large sheets of robust card
- Paints, paintbrushes and paint tray
- Scissors
- Cable ties
- 4 poles
- Ground sheet
- Bunting and flags
- Shields
- Cushions
- Tapestries
- 2 chairs (thrones)

What you do:

1. Decorate four large sections of card with a brick design and create the merlon and embrasure (the teeth at the top of your castle) along the top edges.
2. Cut out an arched doorway in one of the sections of card, and add a few arrow loops (thin slit windows) to all four.
3. Outside, push four poles into the ground in a square or rectangle (or secure the poles on the floor inside, if you would prefer for the den to be indoors).
4. Attach the card around the poles to form the four sides of the castle (cut small slits into the joining edges of the cardboard walls and thread cable ties through the slits and around the poles).
5. Drape with bunting, flags and shields.
6. Inside the castle, cover the floor with a ground sheet, and cushions and hang tapestries on the interior walls. If you have enough room, also include two 'thrones'.

Props and costumes:

What you need:
- ▶ Long skirts, loose-fitting trousers, long-sleeved tops or tunic tops
- ▶ Waistcoats and ribbon
- ▶ Headscarf or wimple hat
- ▶ Flat plain canvas shoes
- ▶ Robe or cloak, wide belt
- ▶ Black boots
- ▶ Tabard and shield
- ▶ Baskets
- ▶ Tankards
- ▶ Wooden plates and spoons
- ▶ Pestle and mortar

What you do:

1. In medieval times, women often wore longs skirt, blouses with long sleeves and corsets. To create a comfortable corset, adapt a waistcoat by adding ribbons and tying at the back! For those working in the castle, add a waist-apron and cap.

2. Male clothes differed depending on status and occupation. Poor men wore basic trousers and shirts and perhaps a hood or hat, whilst noblemen wore clothes made from rich fabrics and cloaks trimmed with fur.
3. Knights wore the archetypal tabard with a design on the front, or full body armour.
4. Props could include items for a feast or a selection of suitable toys, so a 'games' tournament can be enjoyed!

Activities and Games:

What you need:
Crowns
- Thin card
- Colouring pens/pencils
- PVA glue
- Flat back jewels

Tapestries
- Large sheets of paper

Queek Game
- Piece of chequered fabric
- Small stones

Games Tournament
- Marbles
- Quoits/hoopla
- Cup and ball

What you do:
Crowns
Print templates onto thin card (see links opposite). Cut out, colour in and add further decoration with the stick-on jewels. Bend the card in a curve and stick in place.

Tapestries
Castles were cold places, so tapestries showing scenes featuring mythical animals or medieval life were hung on walls. Encourage the children to draw their own tapestries on paper.

Queek Game

To play you will need two or more players. Place the chequered fabric on a flat surface. Before the player throws a stone onto the fabric they guess if the stone will fall on a light or dark square. They gain a point each time they guess correctly. The first player to reach a predefined number (perhaps five or ten) is the winner.

Games Tournament

Encourage the children to enjoy games that medieval children would have played, including marbles, quoits and cup and ball.

Useful links for additional resources:

- ▶ www.castles.me.uk - history of castle and information on life in a castle
- ▶ www.castles-of-britain.com - click on 'castle learning centre' for information on life etc. in a castle
- ▶ www.firstpalette.com - type 'crowns' in the search field for printable templates
- ▶ www.activityvillage.co.uk - type 'knight' in the search field for knight-related resources

Roman Villa

Travel back in time and enjoy the pampered life of rich Roman aristocrats in their Roman villa!

Make and dress your den:

What you need:
- 4 poles
- 2 white sheets
- Cable ties
- Wooden bench
- Cushions
- Decorative carpet (to act as mosaic)
- Fake fur blanket
- Picture of gods, mythical creatures or roman life to hang on walls (alternative to frescos) or draw your own
- Sticky tape

What you do:
1. Push the poles into the ground outside (or secure them on the floor inside, if you would prefer for the den to be indoors).
2. Wrap the sheets around (leaving a gap to serve as a door) and hold in place with the cable ties.

3. Place the carpet on the floor then dress the den with the bench, cushions and fake fur blanket.
4. Dress with other items such as eating implements for use during a great feast.

Props and costumes:

What you need:
- Long white sheets to be wrapped as togas or tunicas
- Alternative: simple white clothing
- Belts and brooches
- Sandals
- Large strips of bright fabric
- Small table
- Bowls, jugs and glasses
- Fruit
- Scroll of paper

What you do:
1. Men: wore either a tunica or a toga. The tunica (short woollen garment with short sleeves) was worn with a belt and was the garment of choice around the house. This could be created using a white sheet and a strip of fabric for the belt. Coloured fabrics would also be draped over the shoulder.
2. Women: also wore a tunica made from two pieces of fabric, which looked like a sleeveless dress. It was held in place with two brooches and a belt. Married women also wore a form of shawl called a 'pulla'.
3. Props could consist of eating implements, which can be used during a great feast.
4. A scroll of paper can be used to read from during speeches.

Activities and Games:

What you need:
- Thin white card and pencils
- Glue stick and scissors
- Small squares of coloured paper
- Thin green card (different shades)
- Plasticene

What you do:
Mosaic
Draw a basic shape or design, e.g. sun rising over the sea, on the thin card. Stick the squares of coloured paper onto the card, keeping within the outline of the picture.

Laurel wreath crown
Cut a strip of white card that is approximately 25cm (1 inch) wide and long enough to go around the head with a small overlap. Curve the card in a circle and stick the two ends together. Cut lots of leaf shapes from the varying shades of green card. Stick the leaves randomly over the white card.

Knucklebones game
Break the plasticene into five small sections and mould into five shapes that roughly represent a sheep's anklebones/ hocks (which were originally used for this game). To play: throw the knucklebones into the air, quickly turn your hand palm-side down and try to catch as many as you can. With each round, the player to catch the most is the winner. Other rules of play can be found on line or in games books.

Useful links for additional resources:
- www.bbc.co.uk/schools/primaryhistory/romans - a brief history of Roman life
- www.historylearningsite.co.uk - information on all aspects of Roman life
- www.teachingideas.co.uk - hover over the 'history' button and click on 'Romans' for resources

Tree House

Every child would love to have a 'proper' tree house and live among the broad branches of a tree. So give them a taster and build a tree house themed den.

Make and dress your den:

What you need:
- Bamboo fencing or screen
- Poles
- Cable ties or tent pegs
- Camouflage fabric
- Cushions and blankets
- Play mats or ground sheet
- Wooden 'furniture', e.g. large logs, can be used as seating

What you do:
1. Push the poles into the ground outside to form a square.
2. Wrap the bamboo screening around the poles, leaving a gap to serve as the door and fix in place using the cable ties.
3. Drape with the camouflage fabric.
4. Cover the interior floor with ground sheet or play mat.
5. Add the blankets and cushions.

Props and costumes:

What you need:
- Everyday clothes suitable for mucky play
- Tree-themed books and posters, including tree identification books
- Fruit from wild trees e.g. acorns, chestnuts, hazel nuts etc.

What you do:
1. Normal clothing can be worn; however, as play is outside then clothes suitable for mucky play are ideal.
2. Props could include a tray for collecting leaves, magnifying glass, microscope, identification books etc., plus insect-catching equipment.

Activities and Games:

What you need:

Learning Leaves
- Selection of leaves
- Laminate sheets
- Scissors

Leaf Printing/ Rubbing
- A5 piece of thick card
- Selection of leaves
- PVA glue
- Paper and crayons
- Paint, paintbrushes, paint tray and foam roller

Story Time
- Tree or leaf-themed picture books

Leaf Bunting
- Dried leaves
- Hole punch
- Large wooden beads
- String

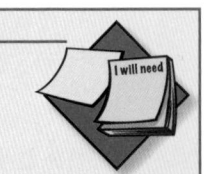

What you do:

Learning Leaves

Laminate a selection of different leaves then use them for a range of activities. For example, place into groups based on size, shape or colour, or use them for counting games.

Leaf Printing/ Rubbing

Cover one side of the thick card with glue, then stick the leaves randomly over the card with the veins face up. Cover again with a layer of glue and allow to dry. Cover with a thin coat of paint, place a piece of paper over the top and gently rub over. Finally peel back to see the leaf pattern created. Alternatively, place thin paper over the leaf-covered card and create a rubbing using a crayon.

Story Time

Enjoy sharing one or two of the many wonderful picture books that feature leaves as their theme.

Leaf Bunting

Cut a length of string to the desired length. Punch holes in the leaves near the stalks. Thread a bead onto the string and tie a knot to hold in place at the end. Thread the other beads and leaves randomly onto the string to create your bunting.

Useful links for additional resources:

- www.sunhatsandwellieboots.com - click on 'nature play' for activity/craft ideas
- http://theimaginationtree.com - type 'nature play ideas' in the search field for activity/craft ideas
- www.forestry.gov.uk - type 'nature play' in the search field for play/activity ideas

Health and safety tips:

- If you choose to capture insects to look at, take great care during the catching and looking process and ensure you carefully release them back where they came from.

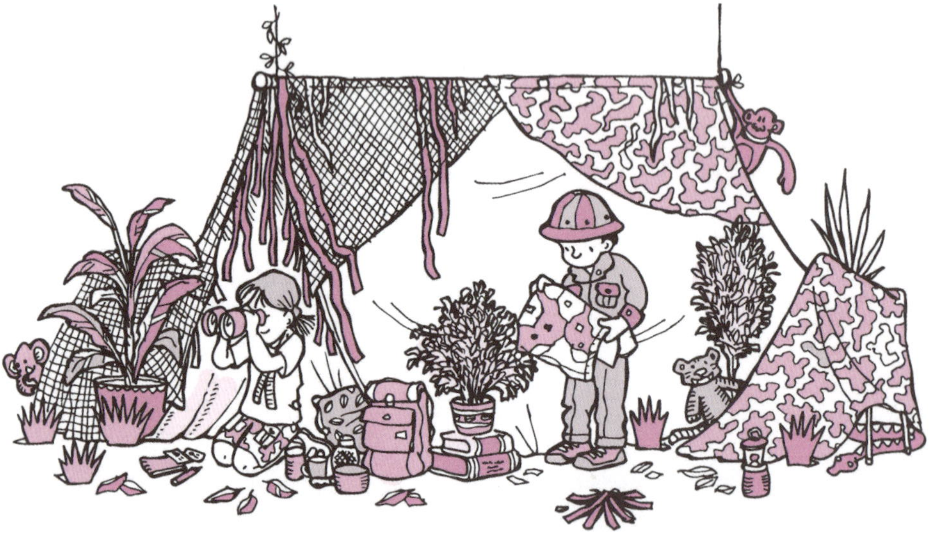

If you have found this book useful you might also like ...

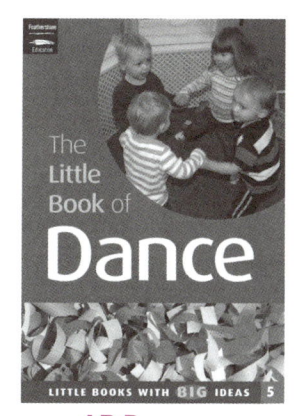

LB Dance
ISBN 978-1-9041-8774-5

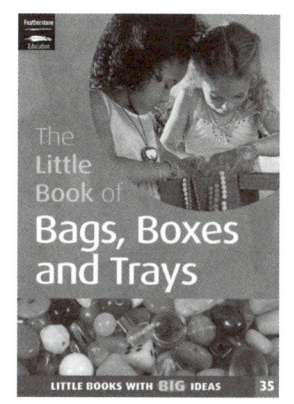

LB Bags, Boxes and Trays
ISBN 978-1-9050-1909-0

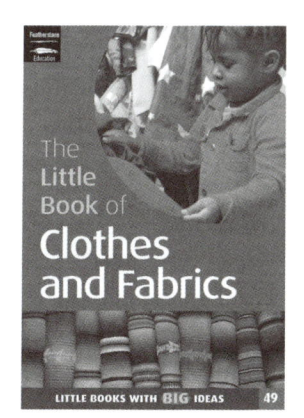

LB Clothes and Fabrics
ISBN 978-1-9050-1969-4

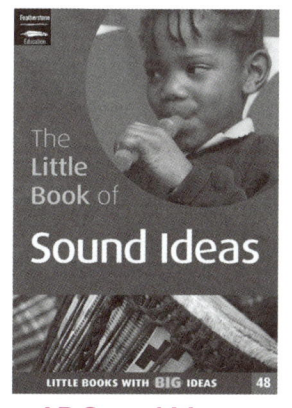

LB Sound Ideas
ISBN 978-1-9050-1955-7

All available from
www.bloomsbury.com

More titles in the Little Books series include ...

LB Making Poetry
ISBN 978-1-4081-1250-2

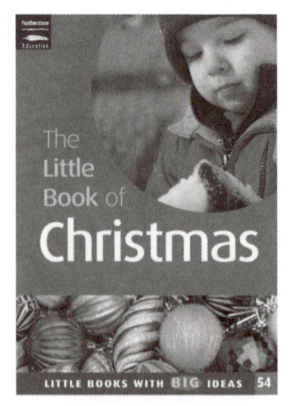

LB Christmas
ISBN 978-1-9022-3364-2

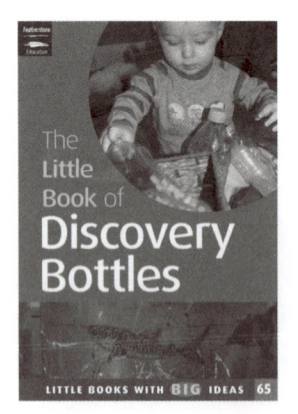

LB Discovery Bottles
ISBN 978-1-9060-2971-5

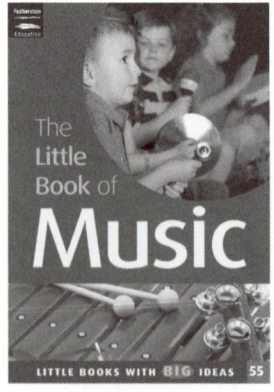

LB Music
ISBN 978-1-9041-8754-7

All available from
www.bloomsbury.com

The Little Books Club

There is always something in Little Books to help and inspire you. Packed full of lovely ideas, Little Books meet the need for exciting and practical activities that are fun to do, address the Early Learning Goals and can be followed in most settings. Everyone is a winner!

We publish 5 new Little Books a year. Little Books Club members receive each of these 5 books as soon as they are published for a reduced price. The subscription cost is £29.99 – a one off payment that buys the 5 new books for £4.99 instead of £8.99 each.

In addition to this, Little Books Club Members receive:
- Free postage and packing on anything ordered from the Featherstone catalogue
- A 15% discount voucher upon joining which can be used to buy any number of books from the Featherstone catalogue
- Members price of £4.99 on any additional Little Book purchased
- A regular, free newsletter dealing with club news, special offers and aspects of Early Years curriculum and practice
- All new Little Books on approval - return in good condition within 30 days and we'll refund the cost to your club account

Call 020 7458 0200 or email: littlebooks@bloomsbury.com for an enrolment pack. Or download an application form from our website:

www.bloomsbury.com

The **Little Books** series consists of:

50	Kitchen Stuff	Puppets in Stories
All through the year	Language Fun	Resistant Materials
Bags, Boxes & Trays	Light and Shadow	Rhythm and Raps
Big Projects	Listening	Role Play
Bricks & Boxes	Living Things	Role Play Windows
Celebrations	Look and Listen	Sand and Water
Christmas	Making Books and Cards	Science through Art
Circle Time	Making Poetry	Scissor Skills
Clay and Malleable Materials	Maps and Plans	Seasons
	Mark Making	Sequencing Skills
Clothes and Fabric	Maths Activities	Sewing and Weaving
Colour, Shape & Number	Maths from Stories	Small World Play
Cooking from Stories	Maths Outdoors	Sound Ideas
Cooking Together	Maths Problem Solving	Special Days
Counting	Maths Songs & Games	Stories from around the world
Dance	Messy Play	
Dance Music CD	Minibeast Hotels	Story bags
Dens	Multi-sensory Stories	Storyboards
Discovery Bottles	Music	Storybuilding
Dough	Nursery Rhymes	Storytelling
Drama from Stories	Opposites	Time and Money
Explorations	Outdoor Play	Time and Place
Fine Motor Skills	Outside in All Weathers	Topsy Turvy
Free and Found	Painting	Traditional Tales
Fun on a Shoestring	Parachute Play	Treasure Baskets
Games with Sounds	Persona Dolls	Treasure Boxes
Gross Motor Skills	Phonics	Tuff Spot Activities
Growing Things	Playground Games	Washing lines
ICT	Prop Boxes for Role Play	Woodwork
Investigations	Props for Writing	Writing
Junk Music	Puppet Making	

All available from
www.bloomsbury.com